THE SECRET LIVES OF LOSERS

by

Megan Mostyn-Brown

FOUNDED 1830

New York Hollywood London Toronto

SAMUELFRENCH.COM

IMPORTANT BILLING AND CREDIT REQUIREMENTS

All producers of THE SECRET LIVES OF LOSERS *must* give credit to the Author of the Play in all programs distributed in connection with performances of the Play, and in all instances in which the title of the Play appears for the purposes of advertising, publicizing or otherwise exploiting the Play and /or a production. The name of the Author *must* appear on a separate line on which no other name appears, immediately following the title and *must* appear in size of type not less than fifty percent of the size of the title type.

THE SECRET LIVES OF LOSERS was originally produced as part of the UMKC Theatre "Festival of N.O.W." for the development of New Original Work at the H&R Block City Stage at Union Station in Kansas City, Missouri on February 10, 2006. The production was directed by Meredith McDonough with the following cast and creative team:

NEELY... Anna Safar
ALEX..TJ Chasteen
SYLVIA.. Angela Cristantello
DJ..Patrick Du Laney
NELSON..Jason Reynolds

VOICE OF JESSICA................................ Cassandra Schwanke
VOICE OF BINGO ANNOUNCER........... Rodney R. Donahue
VOICE OF MRS. WINKLESTEIN.............. Dr. Felicia Londré

Production Manager.. Ron Schaeffer
Assistant Director....................................... Rodney R. Donahue
Scenic Designer.. Jeff Roudabush
Costume Designer................................... Antonia Ford-Roberts
Lighting Designer... Rocco D'Santi
Sound Designer.. .... Rusty Wandall
Technical Director.. Mitch Critel
Stage Manager.. Heather L. Little
Assistant State Managers.......... Jessie Davis, Lauren Lubrow, Genevieve Serville

CHARACTERS

NEELY — 19, works at Amoco, sarcastic, lost

ALEX — 19, small time drug dealer, Neely's best friend

SYLVIA — 19, overly friendly, small town girl, Alex's
      new interest

DJ — 29, cop from Chicago, overweight

NELSON — 15-17, Neely's brother, crystal meth addict,
      sweet but out of control

SOPHIE — Alex's baby, should be a doll in a car seat

JESSICA — Alex's ex-girlfriend, voiceover

SETTING

Small town Illinois, the present

For Salvatore Inzerillo

PROLOGUE

(In blackout we hear the voices of old ladies and a very bored bingo announcer announcing numbers "B12, I 17, O 25" etc... An old lady yells, "Bingo!")

NELSON. Fuck!!!!

SCENE 1

(Lights up on NEELY and ALEX, both 19. They sit on a porch with Sophie, a baby in a car seat. NEELY wears her Amoco polo. ALEX wears a t-shirt that says "Stare at me long enough and I might do a trick".)

NEELY. ... Love. Mom

ALEX. That's it? "I miss you. Love. Mom". The woman's been gone for like two years and that's still all she can write?

NEELY. I guess. Whatever...

ALEX. Where's the postcard from?

NEELY. Bolivia.

ALEX. Where the fuck is that?

NEELY. Dunno like South America or something.

ALEX. Why woudja wanna go there?

THE SECRET LIVES OF LOSERS

NEELY. It looks all green and lush on the card.

ALEX. Well whatever I heard it sucks there anyway.

NEELY. From who?

ALEX. No one specific... It's just like the word on the streets...

NEELY. Ha. Ha.

ALEX. I'm serious if you're like "blah, blah, blah I'm going to Bolivia," anyone would be like, "dude don't go there it sucks."

NEELY. Thanks.

ALEX. No problem. Dija tell yer brother?

NEELY. Fuck no. I told you I never show him any of her postcards.

ALEX. Smart move. Oh shit speaking of yer brother I heard he-

NEELY. Can we not talk about my family today?

ALEX. Sure, whatever... *(Noticing Neely's bulging pockets.)* What the fuck is in yer pants?

NEELY. Oh! Presents...

(She starts to empty her pockets. She pulls out two packs of menthol smokes, Laffy Taffy, a Slim Jim, two cans of Coke, rolling papers and three packages of Corn Nuts.)

NEELY. *(Grabbing the Corn Nuts and putting them back in her pocket.)* Oh, those are for my brother.

ALEX. Jesus Christ!

NEELY. The manager's on vacation er some shit. Figured I'd stock up while she's gone.

ALEX. She's a hag anyway.

NEELY. All the more reason. Got any weed?

ALEX. Yeah.

(He goes into the car seat where Sophie is sleeping. He pulls out a baggie of weed and begins to roll a joint with Neely's papers.)

NEELY. You keep yer weed in Sophie's car seat?
ALEX. Selling. I sell my weed from her car seat.
NEELY. Oh, I'm sorry that makes it totally okay.
ALEX. It's for her benefit.
NEELY. I'm sure Child Welfare Services would totally agree.
ALEX. God you sound like my fuckin' mother-
NEELY. Roll the joint.
ALEX. She found my stash yesterday and is all like on this yer 19 and you need to learn how to be a responsible parent trip... it's fuckin' bullshit man.
NEELY. And being a small time drug dealer is such a noble profession-
ALEX. Do you want me to charge you for this?
NEELY. No.
ALEX. Then lay off.

(He lights the joint and passes it to Neely.)

NEELY. Oh, shit! I forgot to tell you. Member that cheerleader with the frosted perm Allison Blickers?
ALEX. Who?
NEELY. Allison. The one who got caught blowing Mr. Highland in the staff bathroom junior year?
ALEX. Camel toes?

THE SECRET LIVES OF LOSERS

NEELY. No camel toes' best friend.

ALEX. Oh yeah. What about her?

NEELY. She's massively preggers.

ALEX. By Mr. Highland?

NEELY. No, even better dude, Brian Macowski.

ALEX. That stupid fuck who played the flute?

NEELY. Yeah. Can you believe it?

ALEX. Oh my god... Does she still wear those fuckin' leggings?

NEELY. Yeah she had purple ones on underneath her maternity shirt.

ALEX. Oh that's nasty... God, I used to think she was so hot.

NEELY. Not anymore. She's like a major Shamu.

ALEX. I am soooo glad I do not have that life dude.

NEELY. What the fuck'er you talking about? You so do have that life. But like worse.

ALEX. No I don't.

NEELY. Yeah you do. Yer like the pitch for some bad reality TV show on Fox er somethin'.

ALEX. Fuck off! At least I'm not a flute playin' fag.

NEELY. True, true. Speaking of the wicked witch of the mid-west have you heard from Jessica?

ALEX. She's supposed to be coming today... for the weekend.

NEELY. That'll happen.

ALEX. No she is.

NEELY. This was confirmed by her or her mother?

ALEX. Her mother but-

NEELY. You know she only says that shit so you won't call her at school.

THE SECRET LIVES OF LOSERS

ALEX. Shut up. Just shut up okay? You like don't know the first thing about it. *(Sophie starts to cry.)* See now you made the baby fuckin' cry.

(He lights a cigarette and half-hazardly starts to rock the car seat.)

NEELY. Blah, blah, blah I did not make the baby cry. All she does is cry. My point is from personal experience they leave and they don't come back.

ALEX. Jessica is going through college. Not a midlife crisis. *(The baby stops crying)...* Jesus, Finally.

NEELY. Whatever. I'm just suggesting you might try moving on.

ALEX. What time is it?

NEELY. Like 6:30 er somethin'. Why?

ALEX. She's comin' soon. I gotta make sure I have time to put Sophie in that pink baby suit thing with the bows on it that my mom bought her.

NEELY. I wouldn't bust a nut over it.

ALEX. Her mom said they would stop by on the way home from the train station.

NEELY. When hell freezes over.

(She rolls another joint.)

ALEX. Naw like I made her mom promise.

NEELY. In seven months of being at school has Jessica ever once actually showed up to see Sophie? *(Pause.)* And how many times have you sat here for hours on a half assed promise that she would? *(Pause.)* I thought so. *(Sophie starts to whim-*

THE SECRET LIVES OF LOSERS

per.) Look I'm gonna go home and see if my brother's set any-thing on fire. Call me later.

(NEELY EXITS. ALEX pushes the baby away who starts to cry. He puts his head in his hands. Lights down.)

SCENE 2

(Later that night. NEELY'S living room. It looks as if it has not been cleaned in years. The TV blares "Wheel of Fortune". Nelson, 15, NEELY'S brother, is high on crystal meth. He is sweating and shaking. He drinks a Yoo-Hoo and eats Corn Nuts. Bingo cards are spread out on the table amongst the mess of ashtrays, candy wrappers and old newspapers. The room is dark, as the heavy curtains are closed. NEELY ENTERS. NELSON does not notice.)

NELSON. *(To the television.)* Oh shit, oh shit, oh shit you are such a fuckin' dumbass Dave from Utah you shoulda guessed a fuckin' "P"...
NEELY. Nelson.
NELSON. It's obvious, obvious the answer is "Happy Days", "Happy Days", "Happy Days"...

(As he does not acknowledge her, NEELY shrugs her shoulders and quickly and quietly goes to the closet upstage, unlocks it with a key from around her neck and puts the postcard

THE SECRET LIVES OF LOSERS

from her mother and a small framed picture in the closet and then sits in the recliner.)

NELSON. You know I gotta practice- practice for when- so- I gotta for when I win-

NEELY. Nelson.

NELSON. You know I'm gonna win- gonna win start at Bingo work up- end up-

NEELY. Nelson!

NELSON. Oh hey Neels- hey I've guessed like every one answer -every answer- there was this guy-

NEELY. Did you go to school today?

NELSON. Yeah, yeah of course I went I went- like I went in...

NEELY. You went in? Did you stay?

NELSON. Yeah for like a minute, like a long- yeah a long minute but then something came up...

NEELY. What came up?

NELSON. A "Z"? Did you see that? A "Z" who the fuck guesses a "Z"? Stupid fuck-

NEELY. Nelson!

NELSON. Stupid fuckity fuck hee... hee... hee...

NEELY. What came up?

NELSON. Same old shit... Yes! Bankrupt!

NEELY. Nelson what came up?

NELSON. Bitch from Beverly Hills deserves a bankrupt... shit with Mitchell, Mitchell had some shit...

NEELY. Who the fuck is Mitchell?

NELSON. ... You know, you know... the guy he like some- times you know, hooks me up-

NEELY. You got high and left school.

THE SECRET LIVES OF LOSERS

NELSON. Naw naw naw naw naw...

NEELY. Don't lie.

NELSON. Okay so kinda, kinda like a little, like a little...

NEELY. Nelson...

NELSON. I'm cuttin' back swear ta god swear ta god Neels-

NEELY. You can't cut anymore school Nelson.

NELSON. I know I know it's just like temptation like Adam and Eve and the snake and like Mitchell's got like- wow like the shits- the meth's like- and you know, you know-

NEELY. You hafta go. I know it sucks believe me. I know-

NELSON. I know you know I know I mean school is fer chumps.

NEELY. But you gotta go Nelson. I don't wanna get called er nothin' and if they ask me to come in I'll fuckin'-

NELSON. Take a fuckin'- you know take a chill- just chill like they didn't call- they- like no one called-

NEELY. Nelson please go to school tomorrow.

NELSON. I promise, I promise like on time an-

NEELY. -for the whole day-

NELSON. -yeah yeah fer the whole day promise-

NEELY. And no ahh no- just try to lay off the shit you know the-

NELSON. Yeah yeah fer real fer really real can ya, can ya get offa my back I can't hear the show.

NEELY. TV fries yer brain.

NELSON. So does like the ozone, like that ozone layer shit but you still go out in the sun... hee... hee

(Beat.)

THE SECRET LIVES OF LOSERS

NEELY. Nelson. I'm goin' out.

NELSON. Out like a trout. "B" you need ta guess a "B" like fer butthole... hee... hee

NEELY. Don't cause trouble I can't-

NELSON. Yeah, yeah promise with a big "P". No trouble. Later. Later skater.

(He grabs the remote and turns up the television. NEELY stares at him. She throws the Corn Nuts on the table. He watches TV Lights down.)

SCENE 3

(Lights up. It is the next day. NEELY ENTERS. Sylvia Pingerton, 19, sits on the porch with Sophie, who is in her car seat. ALEX is nowhere to be found. SYLVIA wears khaki capris, Keds and a Garfield sweatshirt. She is not that pretty. She is the type of girl who wears dark lip liner with a light lipstick and Lee press on nails. There is a large purse sitting next to her with a grotesque amount of cheesy photo key chains with pictures of cats in them attached to its handle.)

NEELY. Who are you?

SYLVIA. You don't remember? Jesus, it's hasn't even been a year.

NEELY. Since what?

THE SECRET LIVES OF LOSERS

SYLVIA. Since we graduated stupid.

NEELY. *(No clue who she's talking to.)* Uhhh... Janelle?

SYLVIA. No, Sylvia. Sylvia Pingerton.

NEELY. Oh. Shit. You look totally different.

SYLVIA. Yeah I lost like a shitload of weight. Jenny Craig.

NEELY. Yeah... So how have you been?

SYLVIA. You know, cool n' shit. I just moved back from Florida. I was at school.

NEELY. Oh you were at Florida State?

SYLVIA. Naw, community college.

NEELY. You moved to Florida to go to community college?

SYLVIA. I wanted like a change of scenery. And a tan.

NEELY. Oh.

SYLVIA. But like academia wasn't fer me.

NEELY. Guess not.

SYLVIA. Weren't you voted most likely to succeed n' shit?

NEELY. I don't remember.

SYLVIA. Yeah you were. You and that guy Tommy Filmore. They took yer picture fer the yearbook.

NEELY. Oh, yeah.

SYLVIA. So like what the fuck are you up to?

NEELY. I work at Amoco.

SYLVIA. Still? That sucks

NEELY. It's temporary.

SYLVIA. Till what?

NEELY. Till I figure out something not temporary.

SYLVIA. I heard Tommy's at Yale.

NEELY. I guess.

THE SECRET LIVES OF LOSERS

SYLVIA. Weird how shit works out.

NEELY. Why're you here?

SYLVIA. Me n' Alex are going to a movie. Hey, I heard yer little brother's like a major meth head.

NEELY. So it seems.

SYLVIA. That sucks. You know that girl. Who was like a year older than us. She had like brown hair. You know?

NEELY. No.

SYLVIA. Fuck what the fuck's her name. She like worked at the Roll n' Bowl. Anyway, she was a total tweaker. Maybe she knows yer brother.

NEELY. Maybe.

SYLVIA. Anyway, I heard yer mom's like in Bulgaria er some shit.

NEELY. Bolivia.

SYLVIA. That's fuckin wild.

NEELY. I guess.

SYLVIA. My mom, you know, she always said yer mom was like this butterfly trapped in like a dead end chrysalis.

NEELY. What the fuck are you talking about?

SYLVIA. You know she needed to like spread her wings. And fly.

NEELY. You should've been a poet Sylvia.

SYLVIA. Really? Weird. I used to think that about you. Or at least that you'd be really successful even with yer situation at home. Huh... I guess not.

NEELY. Not what?

(SOPHIE starts to cry quietly. SYLVIA rocks her. As SYLVIA is busy, NEELY quickly and quietly slips one of the photos out of one the key chains and slips it into her pocket.)

THE SECRET LIVES OF LOSERS

SYLVIA. Awww iss okay... iss okay Sophiewofey... You know it's so goddam sad. About Sophie. She's fuckin' adorable. I never would have guessed that Jessica Habbermeyer would've you know, run off on her own kid.

NEELY. Well, she was always kind of a cunt.

SYLVIA. No she wasn't she was totally nice.

NEELY. No she wasn't she was totally a cunt.

SYLVIA. God that's like so harsh.

NEELY. So?

SYLVIA. I mean it's just really harsh. Especially when everyone thought she was a sweetie.

NEELY. Fine, fine she was a goddam saint. Look where's Alex?

SYLVIA. He was outta formula. Had to go to the grocery store.

NEELY. Tell'm I stopped by.

SYLVIA. Yeah. Whatever. Oochie-woochie Sophie-wofey.

SCENE 4

(Next day. Spotlight on NELSON US right. On the wall he is spray painting "shitbag cheater" in black. Lights down.)

THE SECRET LIVES OF LOSERS

SCENE 5

(The same day. DJ, a cop age 29 ENTERS the Amoco. He has NELSON, who is squirming, in hand cuffs. NEELY leans behind the counter and reads a magazine.)

NELSON. Hey Neely.

DJ. Is this yer brother?

NEELY. *(Rolling her eyes.)* Yeah.

DJ. I caught him defacing the outside of Sunshine Estates.

NELSON. That old bitch, that old bitch was totally cheating man, totally cheating-

NEELY. The old folks home?

DJ. Yeah.

NELSON. She said those bingo cards were hers but they weren't-

NEELY. So why'd you bring him here?

NELSON. -they weren't they were mine-

DJ. Sandra Shamas said you worked here.

NELSON. -they were on my side of the fucking table-

NEELY. Who's she?

NELSON. -an the fuckin' bitch took 'em Neely!

DJ. The head of the center-

NELSON. Neely!

NEELY. Scuse me. Nelson!

NELSON. What?

NEELY. Shut the fuck up okay? I'm trying to fix this.

NELSON. Okay yeah, yeah okay.

NEELY. *(To N NELSON.)* Thank you. *(To DJ.)*You can uncuff him. He's just high he's not gonna hurt anyone.

NELSON. I'm not high Neel, not that high I mean I only

THE SECRET LIVES OF LOSERS

did-

NEELY. Nelson if you don't be quiet he'll put you in jail.

NELSON. Okayokayokayyeahyeah...

(DJ uncuffs him.)

NEELY. You can grab an icee from the machine an sit in the office. But don't fuck with anything. Okay?

NELSON. Yeahyeahyeah, thanks Neels.

(NELSON EXITS into the back room.)

NEELY. *(Yells into the back.)* And don't fucking smoke pot back there!

DJ. I'm a cop.

NEELY. Duh.

DJ. So you're pretty open about drugs. If he has anything on him I have to-

NEELY. Look clearly you're new here.

DJ. Yeah.

NEELY. Everyone knows my brother's- well it's obvious what he's into.

DJ. Methanphetamines?

NEELY. ANYWAY whatever happened this afternoon we don't got any money to pay for the damage but people are usually pretty understanding and let him do community service. You can write him up if you want but it's just a waste of paper. *(Beat.)* I'm not lying. You can call Sheriff Carlson if you want. He'll tell you the same thing.

DJ. No, no I believe you.

NEELY. Well thanks, you know fer dumpin' him here. *(She*

goes back to reading her magazine.)

(Beat.)

DJ. So what are you gonna do about him?
NEELY. Who?
DJ. Your brother.
NEELY. Ummm... let him sit in the back and watch game shows until I get off.

(She goes back to reading.)

DJ. No, no long term.
NEELY. Long term?
DJ. Well, shouldn't he be in a program or something?
NEELY. Rehab costs a lot of money and he likes to run away.
DJ. Well there are free options-
NEELY. Look do I know you?
DJ. No I just-
NEELY. You just like poking your nose in the business of people you've never seen before Officer.
DJ. DJ. You can call me DJ.
NEELY. Oh um...
DJ. Neely. I know. I've seen you.
NEELY. Where?
DJ. Here.
NEELY. Look I'm pretty familiar with all the cops and I've never seen you.
DJ. Not in here. Driving by. I've seen you when I was driving by. You stare out the window a lot. Like you're looking for

something-

NEELY. Okay I know yer a cop an everything but yer bein' really creepy.

DJ. Sorry.

NEELY. Like stalker creepy.

DJ. I didn't mean it that way. You just seem interesting.

(There is a large crash from the back room.)

NEELY. Fuck! Nelson what the hell are you doing back there?

NELSON. *(From the back.)* Sorry, sorry, sorry. I was jusss tryin' to turn on the TV.

NEELY. I told you not to touch anything!

NELSON. I know, I know I fergot an I stood on the desk and the shelf fell.

DJ. Does he need help?

NEELY. *(Mumbling to herself.)* My life fucking sucks.

DJ. Maybe I should-

NEELY. He does shit like this all the time. *(To NELSON.)* I will be back there in a sec...

DJ. Maybe I should help him.

NEELY. ... fuckin' sit on yer hands er somethin' *(To DJ.)* What?

DJ. Maybe I should help him.

NEELY. No, no. *(There is another crash in the back room.)* Jesus. He is such a fucking mess. *(To DJ.)* Hate ta break off the stimulating conversation but I gotta-

(She turns to leave.)

DJ. Do you wanna go out tomorrow night?

NEELY. What?

NELSON. Neely!

NEELY. *(To Nelson.)* HOLD ON! *(To DJ.)* Like on a date?

DJ. I guess. Yeah.

NEELY. I guess on a date or yeah on a date?

DJ. Yeah. I'm being creepy again aren't I?

NELSON. Neely the shelf's gonna fall more!

NEELY. No. Well kinda... I just don't usually get asked-

DJ. It doesn't even have to be a date we could just hang out.

NEELY. Uhhh... no.

DJ. Just hang out. Promise.

NELSON. Neely!

DJ. Completely informal. You could even bring your brother.

NEELY. Nelson?

NELSON. Neels!!!

DJ. Yeah if you're worried about-

NEELY. No. I mean I guess... why not? Just without my-

NELSON. Holy shit!

NEELY. -my brother.

(Crash!)

DJ. So you'll go?

NEELY. *(Unsure.)* Yeah... yeah I'll go.

NELSON. I'm fuckin' gettin' crushed back here Neels!

DJ. Tomorrow eight o'clock? Meet you here?

NEELY. Yeah sure, here, eight .

NELSON. Neely ya gotta help me-

NEELY. I gotta-

DJ. Yeah. See ya.

NEELY. See ya. *(To the back room.)* Nelson I swear to fucking god...

(Lights down.)

SCENE 6

(Later that day. Lights up on ALEX, NEELY and SOPHIE. They sit on the porch.)

ALEX. ... and then she like slits his throat and that's the end of the movie.

NEELY. That's retarded.

ALEX. I know that's what I said.

NEELY. I can't believe you spent six bucks on that piece of shit. I could've told you it was gonna suck.

ALEX. Yeah, well you left before I got back and she had her heart set on seeing it.

NEELY. I can't believe you went on a date with Sylvia Pingerton.

ALEX. It wasn't a date. We were just hanging out.

NEELY. Hanging out on a date.

ALEX. Look she paid fer all her own shit. So technically, that's not a date.

NEELY. Fine. Whatever. *(Beat.)* She's like really into cats.

THE SECRET LIVES OF LOSERS

ALEX. I don't know.

NEELY. Yes you do. She was the cat girl.

ALEX. What are you talking about?

NEELY. She used to write I heart kittens on the outside of her notebooks and wear puffy painted tees with ironic cat sayings on them.

ALEX. That was like a long time ago.

NEELY. She was wearing a Garfield sweatshirt yesterday. That's kinda hot.

ALEX. I didn't notice.

NEELY. Did you fuck her?

ALEX. No!

NEELY. Well did you go to her apartment?

ALEX. I dropped her off in the parking lot.

NEELY. I bet she has cat knick knacks and hand towels. She probably even owns four or five of the real thing.

ALEX. Three. She has three cats.

NEELY. Right now she has three. But down the road. I mean we could be talking ten or twelve.

ALEX. Hi, I'm Neely and I'm acting like a jealous girlfriend.

NEELY. I am... I am not acting like a... like a jealous girlfriend. Jesus.

ALEX. Could've fooled me.

NEELY. I'm sorry you took my mocking inquisition the wrong way-

ALEX. Mocking inquisition? What're you practicing for the SAT's?

NEELY. Hello!?Even if Sylvia Pingerton wasn't a formerly obese cat freak I still wouldn't be jealous and you would still be a total head case for hangin' with her.

THE SECRET LIVES OF LOSERS

ALEX. Look she's a nice person. Besides I don't see you going on any dates so shut up.

NEELY. Actually, I have one tomorrow night.

ALEX. With who?

NEELY. This cop who tried to arrest my brother earlier today.

ALEX. You have a date with a cop?

NEELY. I'm shocked myself but yeah...

ALEX. What'd Nelson do this time?

NEELY. He spray painted "Mrs. Winklestein is a shitbag cheater" on the front of Sunshine Estates.

ALEX. The old folks home?

NEELY. Yeah. He's been playing Bingo there every Saturday afternoon.

ALEX. Was he high?

NEELY. Probably.

ALEX. And they let him hang out there?

NEELY. The woman who runs the place feels bad for him. She thinks his "peppy" energy is good for the old people and that maybe he'll lay off the meth if he has something to do.

ALEX. Weird. Who is Mrs. Winklestein?

NEELY. His elderly buddy. Supposedly she "totally copped his bingo technique" and won the German chocolate cake he wanted.

ALEX. What?

NEELY. Exactly.

ALEX. And now yer goin' on a date with the cop?

NEELY. I guess.

(Beat.)

ALEX. What were you thinkin'?

NEELY. Dunno. He was like- whatever. I have nothing better to do. So are you goin' out with Sylvia?

ALEX. No. Jessica's s'posed to show up.

NEELY. Oh come on Alex-

ALEX. Before- Before you give me some fuckin' lecture I ran into her cousin Stephanie at Dairy Queen.

NEELY. The lesbian?

ALEX. No, the other one. And she said Jessica's coming home fer the weekend and plans on stopping by to see me n' Sophie.

NEELY. Tonight?

ALEX. I don't know.

NEELY. You don't know what time or what night?

ALEX. Both.

NEELY. So yer gonna sit here all weekend?

ALEX. I mean I guess.

NEELY. Wasn't she supposed to come Thursday?

ALEX. Yeah but shit came up.

NEELY. Classic. How many times did you call her house?

ALEX. You know, a few times.

NEELY. A few times. A few like two or a few like fifteen? *(Beat. Alex does not answer.)* Oh my God.

ALEX. It's not like that.

NEELY. Her mother told you not to call the house anymore didn't she?

ALEX. Naw I think they got caller ID so they just don't answer when it's me.

NEELY. Can't you get her school number from Stephanie?

ALEX. She said she's not supposed to give it out.

NEELY. And this doesn't phase you?

THE SECRET LIVES OF LOSERS

ALEX. Look she's gonna come. She has to okay? I mean she just has to.

NEELY. And if she doesn't?

ALEX. She will.

NEELY. Well have fun. I'm out.

ALEX. Fine.

(NEELY lingers for a second and then turns to leave. SYLVIA ENTERS.)

SYLVIA. Hi Neely.

NEELY. Hello Sylvia.

SYLVIA. Were you leaving? That sucks.

(SYLVIA sits in NEELY'S porch spot. ALEX is lost in thought.)

NEELY. Actually I was just stretching my legs. Look they're stretched.

(NEELY moves SOPHIE aside and sits on the other side of ALEX.They are all squished. SOPHIE starts to cry quietly. ALEX sighs but does nothing. NEELY looks irritated. SYL-VIA stares at the two of them, gets up grabs the car seat, goes back to where she was sitting and puts the car seat on the other side of her causing them all to move over.)

SYLVIA. I read in Ladies Home Journal that sometimes babies cry when they're teething. Is Sophie teething?

ALEX. I dunno.

SYLVIA. I bet she is. I know just the trick. *(SYLVIA coos as she sticks her hand in the blankets giving Sophie her knuckle to gnaw on. The baby stops crying.)* They just love that you know. Not the end of your finger cuz you could cut their gums with your nail-

NEELY. Sylvia why are you here?

SYLVIA. Alex and I were supposed to hang out.

ALEX. No we weren't.

SYLVIA. Yes we were silly. We made a plan.

ALEX. No we didn't.

NEELY. This feels strange.

SYLVIA. We totally had a plan.

NEELY. The make-up of this, of us sitting here.

ALEX. I don't make plans.

NEELY. Sylvia you have to leave.

SYLVIA. Why?

NEELY. You're throwing everything off.

SYLVIA. I am not.

(Beat.)

SYLVIA. Alex we had a plan.

ALEX. Okay I'm breaking it now.

(Beat. SYLVIA does not leave.)

NEELY. This is the part where you get up an leave.

SYLVIA. This is between me an Alex.

ALEX. Look you don't have to leave we're just not going anywhere.

SYLVIA. That's cool. Besides Sophie seems to be enjoying my company.

NEELY. Well at least-

THE SECRET LIVES OF LOSERS

ALEX. Don't start.

NEELY. I'm not. I was just gonna say at least SOME of us have jobs, you know places to be.

SYLVIA. It's my day off.

NEELY. From where?

SYLVIA. Actually I have a really great job doing the books at Nickerson's Nissan. It really utilizes my math skills.

NEELY. Sounds thrilling.

SYLVIA. Hey speaking of thrilling, didn't yer brother get arrested today?

NEELY. Yes.

SYLVIA. Meridith Borson told me that Brian Addleson said that he heard from his cousin Brianne's boyfriend Chuckie that Nelson set fire to the table of bake goods at the cake walk at the State Fair last year cuz he lost. That musta been rough.

NEELY. Well I heard from Mrs. Williamson who's son Robert is best friends with Josie Halpern who knows your sister Jeanie that you couldn't even-

ALEX. What time is it?

SYLVIA and NEELY. What?

ALEX. What time is it?

SYLVIA. 7:00

NEELY. Why?

ALEX. I'm going inside.

SYLVIA. But we were hanging out.

NEELY. Yeah we were hanging out.

ALEX. I'm going to take a nap.

NEELY. I thought you were waiting for-

ALEX. A twenty minute nap.

(He gets up and goes inside.)

THE SECRET LIVES OF LOSERS

SYLVIA. But...
NEELY. Later Sylvia. *(She gets up and leaves.)*

(Beat.)

SYLVIA. But what about the baby?

(Lights down.)

SCENE 7

(The next day. Lights up on DJ and NEELY. They sit on a park bench. Long pause as they look awkward.)

NEELY. Thanks fer the meal.
DJ. You're welcome.

(Pause. More awkwardness.)

DJ. I got you something.
NEELY. A present? You didn't- *(He hands her a terrarium. In it is a crayfish.)* What is it?
DJ. A crayfish.
NEELY. Oh.
DJ. It's like a little lobster.
NEELY. Yeah it kind of is.

THE SECRET LIVES OF LOSERS

DJ. It reminded me of you.

NEELY. It did?

DJ. Yeah, that's why I bought it.

NEELY. It reminded you of me?

DJ. Yeah.

NEELY. In a good way right?

DJ. Of course. I saw it and I thought of you. In a good way.

NEELY. Cuz it looks like me?

DJ. Oh no, no, no... Its personality.

NEELY. Oh.

DJ. The way it looked at people walking by the tank. How it... uhhh... interacted with the other crayfish. Made me... think of... you...

NEELY. Huh...

DJ. This was a weird gift wasn't it? I can-

NEELY. No, no, no-

DJ. -take it back.

NEELY. I like it. It's weird but I like it. I wish I would've-

DJ. No, it's okay-

NEELY. -gotten you something.

DJ. -it wasn't meant like that.

NEELY. *(Digs in her pocket.)* Here... I have a stick of Juicy Fruit.

DJ. *(He laughs.)* It's a little wrinkled.

NEELY. I think it got washed with my jeans. Sorry. It's probably still got good flavor.

DJ. Thanks...

NEELY. God that was so third grade.

DJ. No, no-

NEELY. Jesus.

THE SECRET LIVES OF LOSERS

DJ. It's cute.

(Awkward pause.)

NEELY. So ahhh... you look real different outta uniform.

DJ. Yeah?

NEELY. Yeah like younger... 'n softer.

DJ. Softer?

NEELY. Um... like gentle. Like yer good with babies or yer real nice to yer mom.

DJ. That's a compliment right?

NEELY. Yeah, yeah it's a good thing.

DJ. Thanks.

(Beat.)

NEELY. So are you?

DJ. What?

NEELY. Nice to yer mom?

DJ. I call her every Sunday. How about you?

NEELY. Um... I dunno.

DJ. Oh.

NEELY. Do you like babies?

DJ. Yeah. Sometimes. My sister has one. Jacob. He's three.

NEELY. I bet you're good with him.

DJ. Yeah. He's a cool kid. You?

NEELY. They shit and cry too much. I don't think I'm gonna have kids.

DJ. That'll change.

NEELY. No it won't.

THE SECRET LIVES OF LOSERS

DJ. You say that now but-

NEELY. So why'd you move here?

DJ. Uhhh... I used to live here when I was younger.

NEELY. And you came back?

DJ. Yeah.

NEELY. Why?

DJ. Look you know where the mall is?

NEELY. Only the epicenter of this shit hole.

DJ. It used to be a farm.

NEELY. Classic.

DJ. Cut the sarcasm for half a second and go with me here.

NEELY. Sorry.

DJ. No problem. But you wanted to know so-

NEELY. So it used to be a farm... and?

DJ. And we used to live there. No animals or anything, but a barn and lake, big fields. It was nice. I guess I just had- my best memories are from there.

NEELY. When'd you move away?

DJ. The summer after I think... Yeah. My parents got divorced and my mom and I moved in with my aunt in Chicago after my dad sold the house.

NEELY. Weird.

DJ. What?

NEELY. I guess I just- you know with yer parents n'all you'd think this place'd do the opposite.

DJ. I guess.

(Beat.)

NEELY. Thass not the only reason you came here.

DJ. You're pretty smart for-

NEELY. An Amoco cashier?

DJ. Yeah.

NEELY. I've heard that one before, thanks. *(Beat.)* So?

DJ. So the rest isn't really first date conversation.

NEELY. Says who?

DJ. Says the people who make rules about first dates.

NEELY. Well I don't see any of them here so spill it.

DJ. So what's the deal with you and Nelson?

NEELY. Diversion. One of my favorite tactics.

DJ. I believe it can only be used once in an exchange.

NEELY. That's fair I guess.

DJ. So?

NEELY. Ummm... no comment.

DJ. Not an option.

NEELY. For real?

DJ. Yeah.

NEELY. You sure?

DJ. I gave you a crayfish.

NEELY. True... but not good enough, I need something better.

DJ. Well then... throwing all dating rules aside...

NEELY. Fine by me.

DJ. My girlfriend left me... and... I guess I... .came here... because... here was the last place I had good memories.

NEELY. Oh.

DJ. So? Your turn.

NEELY. So... my dad died from cancer when I was twelve and my mom decided to find herself in foreign countries a few days after I turned seventeen.

DJ. I'm sorry.

NEELY. Shit happens.

(Beat.)

NEELY. It's not like I'm all on my own ya know. I have this friend... ahhh he's there for me.

DJ. Uhhh... oh. Is he like your boyfriend?

NEELY. No, no... no not, not at all. Strictly ahhh... just friends.

DJ. Oh.

NEELY. He's got a baby with some lame bitch so...

DJ. Yeah.

NEELY. I don't like him like that er anything...

DJ. No. Sure, I completely understand.

(Awkward pause.)

DJ. So what do you do here for fun?

NEELY. Plot ways to get out.

DJ. Haven't made it very far.

NEELY. Yeah, well I'm not the greatest plotter.

DJ. You hate this place.

NEELY. No I- It's just- *(Beat.)* Do you always carry yer gun?

DJ. Huh? Yeah. Cops always do. Habit.

NEELY. Have you ever shot anyone?

DJ. No. Have you?

NEELY. No of course not. I've had the urge to.

DJ. What?

NEELY. I've had the urge to shoot someone... well some people.

DJ. How many people?

NEELY. *(Beat. She counts on her fingers.)* Five. Six. No, just five.

DJ. That's a lot.

NEELY. Almost everyone I know.

DJ. Jesus.

NEELY. Right?

DJ. That's a lot of hostility.

NEELY. I know.

DJ. You should do yoga.

NEELY. Yoga? That's fer faggit hippies who eat tofu.

DJ. I do yoga.

NEELY. No way.

DJ. It keeps you fit.

NEELY. Uhhh no offense but I dunno if it's working so well... you're a little bit... well...

(She gestures to his belly.)

DJ. It keeps your mind fit.

NEELY. If you say so.

DJ. Get up.

NEELY. Why?

DJ. I'm gonna show you somethin'.

(They stand in front of the bench.)

NEELY. What are we doin'?

DJ. Put your arms in the air, together like this and breathe in.

NEELY. Okay wait I'm not-

THE SECRET LIVES OF LOSERS

DJ. Put your arms-

(He puts her arms up for her.)

NEELY. -doing this here.
DJ. -in the air.
NEELY. Not in the park okay?
DJ. We're breathing not masturbating Neely.
NEELY. God. I know but-
DJ. But what? Someone might see you?
NEELY. No. Yes. Look it's weird.
DJ. I'm a big fan of weirdness. Now put your arms in the air. *(Beat. She does.)* Close your eyes put your palms together and your leg like this.

(He stands like a flamingo.)

NEELY. Whaaaat?

DJ. Like this. And breathe into it. *(She does it half-assed and keeps one eye open.)* Close your eyes.
NEELY. Jesus.
DJ. Okay do it again. Breathe. *(They do.)* See... not so bad.
NEELY. Yeah, yeah, yeah.
DJ. Practice that at home
 NEELY. Sure.
DJ. Look we can't hang out if you got all that hostility. I don't wanna be an accomplice to murder or nothin'.
NEELY. *(She smiles.)* Yeah... You're like an anomaly. Like yer not what people would think you would be...
DJ. You took a poll?

THE SECRET LIVES OF LOSERS

NEELY. Yeah, I took a poll.

(Beat. They both laugh kind of nervously. He puts his hand on hers. Beat. They do not look at each other.)

NEELY. What does DJ stand for?
DJ. Donald James.
NEELY. Thanks Donald James.
DJ. For what?
NEELY. Dunno yet. Just cuz.

(Lights out.)

SCENE 8

(Lights up on the porch. It is two days later. ALEX sits with his head in his hands. SOPHIE is in her car seat. Hanging from the awning is a large painted arrow. It has fallen askew. Another large paper hangs above ALEX'S head. It has fallen so the audience cannot see what it says. NEELY ENTERS. She is in her Amoco shirt.)

NEELY. Jesus you look rough.
ALEX. Where were you yesterday?
NEELY. I worked a double.
ALEX. I called you.
NEELY. Like I said, I was at work. Don't bust a nut over it.

THE SECRET LIVES OF LOSERS

(Beat.) What's this?
    ALEX. Don't look at it.
    NEELY. Why not?
    ALEX. Just don't. Please.
    NEELY. No I wanna see it.

(She grabs at the paper. He bats her hand away.)

    ALEX. I said no.
    NEELY. Give me the fuckin' paper.
    ALEX. Neely! *(SOPHIE starts to whimper.)* Look you're makin' the fuckin' baby upset.
    NEELY. Fine then!

(She grabs it off of the awning and hops off the porch.)

    ALEX. Fuck you.

(He carelessly rocks the car seat and lights a cigarette.)

    NEELY. Let's see here. *(She unrolls the large paper. It says "Jessica We Are Right Here" with a large arrow pointing downward.)* Jessica... we... are... right... here. Oh my God!
    ALEX. It was Sunday. I was desperate. Give it back.
    NEELY. This is monumental.
    ALEX. Why?
    NEELY. You have officially sunk to a new low.
    ALEX. Shut up.
    NEELY. You thought she forgot where you lived?
    ALEX. Her cousin said she would come.
    NEELY. You waited all weekend.

THE SECRET LIVES OF LOSERS

ALEX. Yes.

NEELY. *(Sarcastically.)* You know the trek from Evanston is three hours. That's quite the journey when you think about it.

ALEX. Fuck off.

(He grabs the sign and throws it to the other end of the porch.)

NEELY. You got any weed.

ALEX. No.

NEELY. Oh. *(Beat.)* Are you lying cuz I looked at your sign?

ALEX. No.

NEELY. Oh. *(Emptying her pockets.)* I brought more rolling papers n' some other shit. *(She pulls out beef jerkey, two packs of menthols, Laffy Taffy, gum, a Coke, and Corn Nuts.)* Oh, those are for my brother.

(She puts the Corn Nuts back in her pocket.)

ALEX. How was yer date?

NEELY. With the cop?

ALEX. No with Brad Pitt.

NEELY. Ha. Ha.

ALEX. Seriously.

(He grabs the rolling papers, takes weed out of SOPHIE'S car seat and starts to roll a joint.)

NEELY. You said you didn't-

ALEX. So was he cool?

NEELY. Yeah you know... I had fun.

ALEX. Oh.

NEELY. Oh. That's it? Oh. You don't have anything else to say?

ALEX. About what?

NEELY. I dunno... about my date?

ALEX. No. Here.

(He hands her the joint.)

NEELY. Oh. *(Beat. They smoke.)* So do you have plans with Sylvia tonite?

ALEX. Yeah. She's comin' over.

NEELY. She's no Jessica Habermeyer.

ALEX. Quit pourin' the Haterade.

NEELY. I'm just sayin'-

ALEX. Sometimes you say too much.

(NEELY starts to say something. She stops. Smokes more pot and then lights a cigarette.)

NEELY. So ummm... I heard Mrs. Rogers found out that Hakim's dad was sharing Blizzards at the Beacon Road DQ with Hannah McKinley's step mom. She's gonna take the house and their dog grooming business. Pretty wild huh?

ALEX. I guess.

NEELY. And Jessica's cousin, the lesbo, she fucked Alex Scaranado, the guy with the cleft chin who was on the wrestling team, in the parking lot at 31 Flavors on Saturday and now she's questioning her sexuality once again.

ALEX. Oh.
NEELY. Are you okay?
ALEX. No.
NEELY. Oh.

(Pause. They smoke.)

NEELY. Ya know-
ALEX. Just... don't.

(Beat.)

NEELY. Ohhhkay... .I'm gonna go... then. Ya know... my brother doesn't like to watch "The Wheel" without his snacks. *(She doesn't leave yet. Pause. ALEX doesn't say anything. He keeps smoking.)* Bye.

(NEELY EXITS. ALEX looks at SOPHIE. She gurgles. He pushes the car seat to the other end of the porch, puts his head in his hands and starts to cry. Lights down.)

THE SECRET LIVES OF LOSERS

SCENE 9

(The next day. Afternoon. Lights up. NEELY is reading a book behind the register in Amoco. The crayfish sits in its terrarium on the counter. DJ ENTERS in his cop uniform.)

DJ. Hey.

NEELY. Oh hey.

DJ. I just figured I would stop-

NEELY. Yeah thass cool it's not busy.   DJ. -by.

DJ. I hope this isn't weird.

NEELY. No, no.

DJ. Nice place you work at.

NEELY. It's an Amoco.

DJ. No but it's nice.

NEELY. It's fucking lame.

DJ. Okay, but it's temporary.

NEELY. So I tell people.

DJ. Be careful, temporary sometimes ends up being a long time.

NEELY. It won't be. I promise. I have zero desire to be buried in this tacky polo.

DJ. So what's your plan then?

NEELY. Fer the rest of my day?

DJ. No you're life.

NEELY. Woah, no offense, but you sound like my guidance counselor.

DJ. Sorry. I just don't know that much about you.

NEELY. Oh.

DJ. So?

NEELY. Jesus... I dunno.

DJ. Huh?

NEELY. Huh what? I dunno. I never really thought about it.

DJ. Never?

NEELY. No.

DJ. Well what did you want to be when you were little?

NEELY. Big.

DJ. What?

NEELY. Yeah when I was little I juss wanted to be big. Not a kid.

DJ. That's weird.

NEELY. Ohhkaay... what did you want to be? Lemme guess a cop?

DJ. No.

NEELY. No?

DJ. No.

NEELY. So?

DJ. It's embarrassing.

NEELY. I'm all for embarrassment.

DJ. I wanted to be a Hell's Angel.

NEELY. You're joking.

DJ. No, not at all.

NEELY. Why?

DJ. Our neighbor was one. He owned a big shiny Harley and a leather vest. Scorpion Bob-

NEELY. His name was Scorpion Bob?

DJ. Swear. Uhhh... I had a name too.

NEELY. I can't fuckin' imagine-

DJ. Snake on Wheels. I always wanted to be called Snake on Wheels. *(NEELY starts laughing.)* I had this jean jacket when I was ten and I put two patches together on the back, this really mean looking python and a Harley.

 NEELY. You did not?

 DJ. Seriously.

 NEELY. So you became a cop instead?

 DJ. Yeah, well Eric Estrada was my other idol.

 NEELY. Who?

 DJ. He was on CHIPS.

 NEELY. CHIPS?

 DJ. That TV show from the- Never mind.

 NEELY. Okay.

 DJ. So?

 NEELY. So what?

 DJ. So what's your favorite thing?

 NEELY. I dunno.

 DJ. What? Give me a break everyone has a favorite thing.

 NEELY. Apparently I'm not like ev-

(SYLVIA ENTERS.)

 SYLVIA. Neely.

 NEELY. Sylvia.

 SYLVIA. Hello.

 NEELY. Hello.

 SYLVIA. Working?

 NEELY. Obviously.

 SYLVIA. I have gas. *(Beat.)* On pump three. Ten dollars.

 NEELY. Okay.

 SYLVIA. *(Noticing the crayfish.)* Ewww... what's that?

 DJ. A crayfish.

 SYLVIA. *(Noticing DJ.)* Who are you?

 DJ. Uhhhh... I'm a cop.

THE SECRET LIVES OF LOSERS

SYLVIA. Duh. Like yer name. I'm Sylvia.

DJ. Officer Warren.

(SYLVIA looks from NEELY to DJ.)

SYLVIA. Oh shit-are you?

NEELY. Do ya want anything   SYLVIA. Yer the cop she-
else Sylvia-

SYLVIA. - went on a date with aren't you?

DJ. Uhhh...

SYLVIA. It's cool. I know all about it. Al told me.

NEELY. Al? Since when is he Al?

SYLVIA. Since we're like on that kind of name basis.

DJ. Al?

SYLVIA. My-

NEELY. My best friend. And it's Alex.

DJ. Oh, that guy.

SYLVIA. *(To DJ.)* You sound jealous. Don't be. There's nothing between them. *(To crayfish.)* God that fish thing is really ugly.

NEELY. When crayfish lose a leg it regenerates.

SYLVIA. Weird.

NEELY. Humans aren't so lucky.

SYLVIA. Anyway. *(Turning to DJ.)* You're not really what I expected.

DJ. In what way?

NEELY. Do you need anything   SYLVIA. I mean my cousin
else besides the gas?   Elly

SYLVIA. -said there was this new cop from the city and I kept imagining that guy from "Saved By The Bell" was on "NYPD Blue" he's like the hot cop with a past-

THE SECRET LIVES OF LOSERS

NEELY. Sylvia- It's ten dollars. Cash or charge?
SYLVIA. -and yer just well so-
NEELY. Cash or charge?
SYLVIA. I dunno. Big.
DJ. You mean overweight and out of shape.
SYLVIA. Sure I guess. Cash.

(She takes out money and hands it to NEELY.)

NEELY. Sylvia-

(DJ looks at her in an "I can handle it" kind of way.)

DJ. Sylvia you talk a lot.
SYLVIA. I do have the gift of gab.
DJ. It's not a gift.

(NEELY stifles a laugh.)

SYLVIA. Well- I-Whatever- *(Beat. To Neely.)* I'll tell Al you said hi. *(NEELY shrugs and stares at SYLVIA. DJ stares as well.)* Yeah.

(SYLVIA EXITS.)

DJ. Good friend of yours?
NEELY. Yeah. The best.
DJ. I can tell. So-
NEELY. That was cool-how you- what you said to her...
DJ. No problem.
NEELY. She's a total-

DJ. She just needed to be put in her place.

NEELY. I guess. Thanks.

DJ. You're welcome.

(They stare at each other. Awkward pause.)

NEELY. I ummm... really like thunderstorms.

DJ. Huh?

NEELY. My favorite thing... I guess always... is thunderstorms.

DJ. Oh yeah well that's a start.

NEELY. To what?

DJ. I dunno... you could be a meteorologist.

NEELY. That's just as lame as working here.

DJ. You could be a storm chaser.

NEELY. That's ridiculous. Besides there hasn't been a tornado here in like ten years.

DJ. Okay. Let's take another route. You're really good at taking care of your brother.

NEELY. Sometimes. But whatever that's not a choice.

DJ. But you have a lot of patience with him.

NEELY. I have to. Besides he doesn't have anyone else.

DJ. Well, you could put him in-

NEELY. I can't get rid of him like-I just don't believe in doing that to people.

DJ. It's not fair to you.

NEELY. Depends on who's lookin' at the situation. *(She looks behind her out the window.)* There's someone on pump five. So I gotta make like I'm workin'. Sorry.

DJ. No problem.

NEELY. We can hang out again. I mean when we're not

working. If that'd be okay with you?

DJ. Yeah.

(Awkward pause.)

NEELY. Sorry.

DJ. About what?

NEELY. You know buggin' out about Nelson, Sylvia, blah, blah, blah.

DJ. No problem.

NEELY. You make me wanna be honest.

DJ. In a good way?

NEELY. Yeah, in a good way. *(She looks out the window.)* The guys ummm headin' inside so...

DJ. Yeah. *(Beat.)* So maybe this weekend we'll...

NEELY. Yeah. Ummm... have a good day.

DJ. You too. *(Beat. He lingers.)* Neely.

NEELY. Huh?

DJ. I think you know what you want... in life. You're just too afraid to say it.

(Beat. She says nothing.)

DJ. You gotta be the one to exact change. No one else is gonna do it for you. *(Pause.)* See ya.

NEELY. Yeah. See ya.

(DJ EXITS. She watches him leave. Lights down.)

THE SECRET LIVES OF LOSERS

SCENE 10

(Same day. Early evening. Lights up on SYLVIA and ALEX. They are sitting on ALEX'S porch. SOPHIE'S carseat is in SYL-VIA'S lap. She is playing with the baby. ALEX smokes a cigarette and looks sort of happy. NEELY ENTERS. They do not see her.)

SYLVIA. ... and so then I heard they wouldn't let Nelson back in to Sunshine Estates until he got clean cuz he's scaring the old ladies. It's a tragedy really-

ALEX. I guess.

SYLVIA. Right Sopheywofey? Right baby? God she's so cute... .

(NEELY lingers for a moment, takes out all the shit in her pockets she's stolen from work and throws it to the side. She notices the packages of Corn Nuts, picks them back up and stuffs them in her pocket. She watches SYLVIA and ALEX for a moment and then kicks all of her discarded goods out of the way and leaves. Lights out.)

THE SECRET LIVES OF LOSERS

SCENE 11

(Later that evening. The Neilsen living room. NELSON is high and watching "Wheel of Fortune". The living room is in disarray. NEELY ENTERS and sits in the recliner.)

NELSON. Spin it, spin it, spin that wheel. Yes! Okay guess a "d" it's "d" for Partridge Family-

NEELY. Hey Nelson.

NELSON. A "V"? Who are you? It's Partridge like Susan Dey- "be happy"- fuckface- Jesus-

NEELY. Nelson!

NELSON. Now Vanna isn't gonna turn the — fuck- no letter-

NEELY. Nel- Never mind.

NELSON. Oh hey Neels- no one's gonna beat Vera- cuz-

NEELY. That's great Nelson.

NELSON. And Vanna is so- she's the great Neels- she's underrated-

NEELY. Have you been sitting here all day?

NELSON. No... No... Yes-

NEELY. Nelson-

NELSON. No but wait I didn't get inta no trouble- and I had a visitor- a visit from a person-

NEELY. The people on TV don't count-

NELSON. Naw, naw, naw Mitchell-

NEELY. Nelson, you can't invite your drug dealer over-

NELSON. Buy a vowel... Buy an "E" "E" "E"-take a pill er chill- you smoke with Alex outside- Mitchell was inside-

NEELY. Fuck that's different- Nelson I asked you to lay off the-

THE SECRET LIVES OF LOSERS

NELSON. Swear I am-

NEELY. You have to get your shit together Nelson. I can't do it for both of us.

NELSON. I know, I know which is why this-the meth- the Mitchell meth- has me- see there needs to be a sign cuz yer no Vanna-

NEELY. What the fuck are you talking about?

NELSON. Vanna she's just always there turning letters- in sparkly dresses- Pat gets all the credit- but Vanna she makes it happen-no matter what-always there-

NEELY. I'm doing the best I can-

NELSON. She's comforting like a blankee- you had a blankee- me too mine was-mine was blue- member?

NEELY. Yeah, I do.

NELSON. Yer you, yer not Vanna Neels-

NEELY. I'm trying Nelson.

NELSON. -and the meth- there'll be a sign- Buy and "E" —"EEEE"

NEELY. I'm tryin' Nelson. But you've gotta-

NELSON. Shhh- there'll be a sign- cuz yer no Vanna- mom was- maybe Sandra Bitch Shamas-but yer not supposed to turn letters-

NEELY. I dunno about that.

NELSON. Promise it'll be okay- with a "O" a big "O"- fer what I said-

NEELY. Yeah. Hopefully. *(Beat.)* I'm gonna go to bed.

NELSON. Sleep tight-don't let- there's bed bugs that bite-er whatever the fuck.

NEELY. Yeah. Thanks. Oh, I almost forgot. Here.

(NEELY takes the Corn Nuts out of her pocket and places them

on the table. Nelson grabs them and tears into them.)

NELSON. Yer the best- with a "B" for bed.

(NELSON eats. NEELY watches him for a moment. Lights down. In blackout we hear the sounds of a police siren)

SCENE 12

(Next day. Lights up on NEELY and DJ as they sit in the park. She holds her Amoco shirt. He wears his cop uniform. The crayfish terrarium sits on the ground.)

NEELY. So...

(Beat.)

NEELY. I'm so fucking humiliated.
DJ. You should be.

(Pause.)

NEELY. Look. In my defense I never intended to-
DJ. Get arrested?
NEELY. Well, yeah.
DJ. That's a start.
NEELY. My brother he just- he just has this really big ad-

diction to Yoo-hoo and Corn Nuts and we-

DJ. Cut the crap.

NEELY. It's not crap. We don't got alotta money. So I took the shit from work-

DJ. Grow up Neely.

NEELY. I'm serious.

DJ. Are you listening to yourself?

NEELY. Yeah I'm speaking aren't I?

DJ. No but you're not listening. You were just arrested for stealing. Multiple times. And because you're not a minor anymore that means that this goes on your permanent record. And if the manager presses charges you could go to jail.

NEELY. Duh, what the fuck do you think I'm freaking about?

DJ. Do you want to end up like your brother?

NEELY. Stop it.

DJ. No you stop it.

NEELY. Look I called you because I wanted a friend not some fucking militant parent figure.

DJ. Isn't that what you need?

NEELY. Fuck you. You're not all you're cracked up to be.

(NEELY gets up to leave. DJ grabs her.)

DJ. Neely wait-

NEELY. No let-

DJ. Neely-

NEELY. Me go.

DJ. I'm sorry. *(She yanks her arm out of his and sits back down on the bench next to him and then moves farther away.)* I'm sorry.

NEELY. That hurt.

DJ. I didn't mean to grab you that hard.

NEELY. Don't do it again.

DJ. Touch you?

NEELY. No... I mean yes... I mean you can... you can ummm touch me if... if you want... I mean... touching me... that would be nice I guess. Just not like that.

DJ. Oh. *(He goes to put his hand on hers and then decides against it.)* I just wanted you to stay.

NEELY. Well, I'm here.

DJ. Then can we talk about this?.

NEELY. Maybe you should start talking.

DJ. This isn't about me.

NEELY. Yeah well maybe it should be. I'm not the only person who's been hiding something.

DJ. What the hell are you talking about?

NEELY. I overheard some shit at the police station.

DJ. From who?

NEELY. It's a small town, people talk.

DJ. Well whatever they were talking about has nothing to do with me and you.

NEELY. I think it does. You lied.

DJ. Lied about what?

NEELY. Why did you leave Chicago?

DJ. My girlfriend left me.

NEELY. She wasn't your girlfriend.

(Beat.)

DJ. Shit... okay... she was... ummm... my wife. And I just thought it was... weird... telling you that I was married.

THE SECRET LIVES OF LOSERS

NEELY. Um I'm sorry but it's weirder to NOT tell me you're married.

DJ. I'm not married anymore... technically.

NEELY. Since she's technically not here? Jesus-

DJ. She's not coming back.

NEELY. Yeah, right.

DJ. Believe me she's not.

NEELY. Why?

DJ. Since when did you become Barbara Walters?

NEELY. Since you started being shady.

DJ. She was a coke addict. It's not that interesting of a story.

NEELY. Seemed like it at the precinct.

DJ. Well we're not at the precinct and I think that what's going on with you is a little more relevant.

NEELY. I'm not sayin' shit till you to tell me the truth.

(Beat.)

DJ. Jesus... ahhm... my wife... I mean ex-wife Berniece...

NEELY. *(Starting to laugh.)* Berniece?

DJ. Don't laugh at her fucking name or I'm not gonna finish...

NEELY. I'm not laughing. No one's laughing.

DJ. Berniece... she wasn't an addict when I met her... It was something that developed over the years... .My partner arrested her buying drugs on Howard Street... ummm... I bailed her outta jail and she emptied our bank account, maxed our credit cards and left town... After that I-

NEELY. Ran away.

DJ. I did not run away.

THE SECRET LIVES OF LOSERS

NEELY. Sounds like it to me.

DJ. Look my life was never supposed to be that. I think you can relate. *(Beat.)* I didn't tell you because I was embarrassed.

NEELY. That she was a drug addict?

DJ. No... that I let her be one... I'm a fucking cop and I didn't do anything about it.

(Beat.)

NEELY. Do you wish you had her back?

DJ. Honestly?

NEELY. Honestly.

DJ. Some days, yeah I guess.

NEELY. Even if she was inta the same shit?

DJ. *(Very quietly.)* Yeah.

(Beat.)

NEELY. Yeah me too. About my mom... not Berniece no offense.

DJ. Wait your mom wasn't...

NEELY. No, no, no, no... she was artsy fartsy.

DJ. Arsty fartsy?

NEELY. Yeah she was inta dumb shit like decoupage and dream catchers. *(Beat.)* I guess she wasn't cut out fer bein'...

DJ. It's okay to hate her.

NEELY. Puhleeze. I have no problem doing that.

DJ. You sure?

NEELY. Yeah.

DJ. She's the reason you're here right now.

NEELY. I am here right now because I got busted lifting

THE SECRET LIVES OF LOSERS

shit from work.

DJ. It's a repercussion of something else.

NEELY. Don't give the bitch too much credit.

DJ. Stop acting like a kid and look at the bigger picture.

NEELY. Bigger picture? Right. By the way, what are you doing that's so fucking fabulous?

DJ. I took a chance. I saw that my life wasn't working the way it was and I took a chance.

NEELY. No you came to reclaim some childhood memory that doesn't even exist because it was replaced by Marshall Fields and 5-7-9.

(Beat.)

DJ. Wow... well if that's what you think... uhhh... I should go.

(He gets up to leave.)

NEELY. Fuck! No, wait! Don't go. I shouldn't have said that about the mall. It was low. Swear ta God no more wise cracks. Just don't go okay? *(Pause. They look at each other.)* I uhhh... I don't have... anyone else... to... go to.

DJ. What about that guy?

NEELY. Alex? He's ummm... he's umm busy with Sylvia er somethin' ...

DJ. Okay. Fine. Then what're you gonna do to change things?

NEELY. *(Sadly.)* I'm trying.

DJ. No you're not.

NEELY. I am though.

DJ. You don't have a job anymore. Do you understand what that means?

NEELY. The manager was a bitch anyway.

DJ. That's not the point-

NEELY. And you should know she's been importing discount smokes from the Czech Republic and selling them for cheap-

DJ. They could take away your brother because of this.

NEELY. Good! *(Beat.)* Fuck I didn't... really... mean it to come out that-

DJ. Then look inside and figure something out instead of making jokes to hide the fact you're stalling in someone else's shit.

NEELY. I swear I only do it at work. And it was just some little shit for fun-

DJ. You're far too complicated for that.

(Beat.)

NEELY. I am?

DJ. Oh yes.

(Beat.)

NEELY. Can I tell you something?

DJ. Sure.

NEELY. *(Quietly.)* I just... I just wish someone would tell me what I'm supposed to do.

DJ. I wish someone would tell me what to do too.

NEELY. I meant that seriously.

DJ. So did I.

NEELY. Oh.

(Beat.)

NEELY. I'll change. Promise.
DJ. You don't have much of a choice now do you?

(Silence. They sit. NEELY looks as if she might cry. Blackout.)

SCENE 13

(Later that evening. Lights up on NEELY and NELSON'S living room. It is in more disarray as NELSON has found boxes of cataloged items which are spilling out and all over the room from a closet upstage. "Wheel of Fortune" blares in the background. NELSON is nowhere to be found. NEELY ENTERS with the crayfish.)

NEELY. Nelson I got fi- *(Notices the mess.)* Oh fuck! Oh fuck! How did he get the lock open!? *(She tries pushing all of the stuff back into the closet. There is too much. We hear a toilet flush.)* Dammit.

(She pushes the chair against the other door so NELSON can't get out.)

NELSON. *(From inside the bathroom.)* Neely? Neels? Hey

THE SECRET LIVES OF LOSERS

I can't get out.

NEELY. *(Still trying to put the stuff away.)* Fuck fuck fuck fuck fuck fuck fuck!!!

(Her swearing continues under NELSON'S lines.)

NELSON. Neely? Guess what? I found shit I found some fuckin' dope shit dope shit tons of dope shit right here like a treasure... a treasure sign... Neely? *(She gives up grabs the crayfish and EXITS.)* Neels? Neels?

(Lights out.)

SCENE 14

(The next day, NEELY sits on the awning of ALEX'S porch. She holds the crayfish in its terrarium. She has been waiting there all night. ALEX comes up the walk with SOPHIE in her car seat.)

ALEX. What are you doing up there?
NEELY. Where were you all night?
ALEX. What are you doing up there?
NEELY. Exacting small amounts of change.
ALEX. What?
NEELY. Come up.
ALEX. No. Get down.

THE SECRET LIVES OF LOSERS

NEELY. C'mon Alex.

ALEX. What are you holding?

NEELY. My crayfish.

ALEX. What?

NEELY. My crayfish.

ALEX. Have you dipped into yer brother's stash er some shit?

NEELY. No. I'm totally sober.

ALEX. Get down before my mother comes home.

NEELY. She went to work an hour ago. Come up.

ALEX. Well, I have a baby.

NEELY. So?

ALEX. Neely It's fucking nine AM, I'm exhausted and totally not interested in your bullshit right now.

NEELY. Where were you all night?

ALEX. Out.

NEELY. You were at Sylvia's weren't you?

ALEX. It's none of your fucking business where I was.

NEELY. You slept at her house.

ALEX. Look I don't even know why we're having this conversation.

NEELY. Because I'm seriously questioning things Alex.

ALEX. Have you lost your mind? Cuz right now yer making no fucking sense.

NEELY. Okay , where do you wanna be in life?

ALEX. What!?

NEELY. Do you wanna be here like doing the same shit ferever?

ALEX. Oh my god... Will you please just get down?

NEELY. Seriously. I'm getting all existential on yer ass just go with me here.

THE SECRET LIVES OF LOSERS

ALEX. Exi what?

NEELY. Existential. Philosophical. Don't you read?

ALEX. The TV Guide.

NEELY. Jesus Christ.

ALEX. And Sports Illustrated.

NEELY. See this is what I mean-

ALEX. And I read that book by that guy from Star Trek... about babies.

NEELY. Dr. Spock?

ALEX. That's it.

NEELY. Jesus Christ Alex!

ALEX. Well what the fuck are you getting at then?

NEELY. Okay... what's the one thing you want more than anything?

ALEX. What? Uhh... .Jessica.

NEELY. That's retarded. Especially when you've been spending the night with Sylvia.

ALEX. I am not getting into this with you. Not today.

NEELY. Fine. What's your favorite thing in the whole world?

ALEX. I dunno...

NEELY. That's not an answer.

ALEX. Well what's yours?

NEELY. Rain.

ALEX. Rain?

NEELY. Not just any kind of rain. Rain when there's a thunderstorm and it hasn't happened yet but you can see it coming... you can see it raining like a mile away. Like in yer car on the freeway.

ALEX. What the fuck is going on with you?

NEELY. How long have we known each other?

THE SECRET LIVES OF LOSERS

ALEX. Neely I am not in the mood fer a fuckin' trip down memory lane.

NEELY. We've known each other since second grade. We've spent every single day together since we were seven. You were at the hospital when my dad died. I was at your house when Jessica dumped you with Sophie-

ALEX. What are you getting at?

NEELY. You stayed at my house for three weeks after my mom bailed.

ALEX. Fuck Neels I am not in the mood fer a psycho freak out-

NEELY. I lost my job yesterday and I called you and you didn't answer and I came by and you weren't here and I sat here all night and waited for you.

ALEX. Look I've been busy. I've got a kid.

NEELY. That's not the point.

ALEX. Then what is the fucking point?!

NEELY. The point is... The point is I always thought that no matter what happened that in the end we would...

ALEX. We would what?

NEELY. We would be...

(Pause. They look at each other.)

ALEX. Just get off the roof Neely.

NEELY. That at the very least there would always be a me n'-

ALEX. Neels, I gotta kid.

NEELY. I know but we could still...

ALEX. Stop it. I gotta kid.

NEELY. Alex, you've never even attempted to visit Jessica

THE SECRET LIVES OF LOSERS

at Northwestern.

(Beat. ALEX is speechless.)

NEELY. Do you even love Sophie?

(Beat.)

ALEX. She's my kid.

NEELY. You don't love her do you?

ALEX. Shut up.

NEELY. You don't feel like she's yours.

ALEX. I said shut up.

NEELY. She's always in her car seat. You don't play with her.

ALEX. You don't see us every second of every day.

NEELY. But you don't do you?

ALEX. Since when have you been so concerned with Sophie's welfare?

NEELY. I'm not. But you're using her as an excuse-

ALEX. An excuse? What about your mother? She seems to be a pretty fucking big excuse for you.

NEELY. At least I can admit I hate her. I HATE MY MOTHER. See, it's not a bad thing.

ALEX. Jesus what is yer point here besides being totally fucking bizarre!?

NEELY. Let her go.

ALEX. Who?

NEELY. Jessica. Let her go. Give up Sophie. Give up-

ALEX. She is coming here later. I told you that.

NEELY. No she's not! Don't you see that?

THE SECRET LIVES OF LOSERS

ALEX. You are such a fucking bitch-

NEELY. And even if she did FINALLY fucking come and visit it wouldn't be like it is in yer head-

ALEX. Yes it would!

NEELY. She doesn't want to be here Alex. She wouldn't be the same if she was here and she would hate you and she would hate Sophie.

ALEX. Shut up!

NEELY. Deep down inside you know it Alex. You know that baby is an excuse because as long as you bear that burden you never have to confront the fact that Jessica is gone for good and that it's time for you to MOVE ON and be something better than a small time drug dealer who bides his time with idiots like Sylvia Pingerton.

ALEX. Shut the fuck up! *(The baby starts crying.)* Shit! Shit! See what you did! Now she's gonna be up all fucking day! God you are so fucking selfish.

NEELY. This isn't about me anymore.

ALEX. Fuck you! God! Please stop crying! *(The baby cries louder.)*

NEELY. Give her up Alex.

(The phone rings inside.)

ALEX. Dammit! *(We hear the answering machine beep.)* JESSICA. Hey Al... Al are you there?

ALEX. Oh my god it's Jessica! Shit.

(He runs in the house leaving SOPHIE on the porch who has quieted down. ALEX can be heard mumbling from inside

THE SECRET LIVES OF LOSERS

the house. Beat. NEELY slides off the roof. She peeks into the door, looks around, grabs SOPHIE'S car seat and EXITS. ALEX reENTERS talking.)

ALEX. She apologized Neely. I told you. She said she's comin' tomorrow if she doesn't have to work on a project- but I feel like tomorrow's gonna be the day- *(Realizes he is alone.)* Neely!

(Lights down.)

SCENE 15

(Same day. Lights up. NEELY and DJ are in the park. She has the crayfish and SOPHIE. DJ is in uniform.)

NEELY. I called the precinct cuz I needed to find you.
DJ. Who's this?
NEELY. Can you take off yer cop shirt?
DJ. You didn't answer my question.
NEELY. Nothin' sexual. I juss - Can you take off yer cop shirt I can't talk to you like this.
DJ. Uh, yeah, okay. *(He takes off his shirt. He is wearing an undershirt underneath.)* Why the hell do you have a baby?
NEELY. It's not mine. It's Alex's.
DJ. I figured. Are you babysitting?
NEELY. No I took it.

DJ. Because he needed a break?

NEELY. No.

DJ. You've suddenly taken a liking to children?

NEELY. No I took it while he was inside.

DJ. He doesn't know?!

NEELY. No.

DJ. Kidnapping Neely? This is considered kidnapping!

NEELY. Okay I did... take Sophie but-

DJ. KIDNAPPED, Abduction. If you think you were in trouble for stealing Slim Jims and Skittles wait till you get slapped with a felony.

NEELY. It's not like that. It's not like that at all.

DJ. I am a cop Neely.

NEELY. Lemme explain.

DJ. You have more than explaining to do.

NEELY. I lied. I lied to you and I'm sorry I lied cuz you've been nothin' but nice. Always.

DJ. Lied about-

NEELY. Everything.

DJ. Everything? Okay. Last we talked you were attempting to make a change.

NEELY. I am, I am I'm totally exacting change all over the place but it just involved a few things that I didn't expect-

DJ. Like kidnapping?

NEELY. Sorta.

DJ. Are you high?

NEELY. No, no. I'm totally sober.

DJ. You're certainly not acting like you are.

NEELY. I'm not. Swear. I juss gotta clear up a few things okay?

DJ. What things?

THE SECRET LIVES OF LOSERS

NEELY. It just- It wasn't fair that I made you say all that shit about Berniece an then I didn't return the favor. I left out some details.

DJ. Details about what?

NEELY. The stealing.

DJ. What is going on with you Neely?

NEELY. Okay so ummm... Right after my mom left Mrs. Finklestein baked us a ziti... she's one of the neighborhood ladies without husbands or children who does that, bakes for us because we have a bad situation and I thank her fer the ziti and she smiles at me like I know she's gonna go to her Stitch n' Bitch meeting the next day and talk about how sad we are and she turns her back and I took it.

DJ. The dish?

NEELY. No the ashes of her terrier Pierre. Slipped the little silver box with the stupid dog clasp into my pocket and walked out the door. She never knew it was me. Did the same thing with Abby Hildreth's dad who kept offering us his lawnmower because our yard was overgrown. Took the only picture of his grandfather off the coffee table. Mrs. Markus's embroidered pillow. Dr. Hildari's passport... etc... etc... I had a whole closet full ah shit.

DJ. How many things?

NEELY. Dunno four or five hundred. Took shit at parties, at school, wherever I thought someone was- Look my life was never supposed to be this way. Did you know I was voted most likely to succeed?

DJ. No.

NEELY. Maybe I coulda gone to Yale just like Tommy Filmore. I guess that's kinda beside the point right now. Anyway-

THE SECRET LIVES OF LOSERS

DJ. What did you do with all of the stuff?

NEELY. My brother got the closet open. It's all over the living room floor.

DJ. Jesus...

NEELY. I got so good at it... the stealing... that I took the stuff at work to fill the mean time. You know, fill in between staking out the meaningful stuff.

DJ. Neely...

NEELY. No. You know, I always felt like- Naw I- I always hoped that when I died they'd open my closet and everyone'd find all their lost shit and this flood of great memories will wash over them as they remember how special these things were to them and in the midst of it they'd umm... .think of me and what they have and not what I don't have.

DJ. Jesus... I'm sorry.

NEELY. No don't say yer sorry. You have nothing to be sorry about.

DJ. Look if I had known what I said was going to-

NEELY. I'm the one who should be sorry.

DJ. For what?

NEELY. For us never gettin' an appropriate second date.

DJ. Oh. Well you've had a lot going on-

NEELY. No, no cuz you've been nothin' but nice even when you didn't seem like you were bein' nice you were. About everything.

DJ. Well thanks, I wanted to... be nice-I like you- a lot- but you- the point of this is- regardless of the other stuff you took you have to bring the baby back. I know you're all messed up about your mom but that's no reason to-

NEELY. I can't.

DJ. It's a baby Neely. You can't store it in a closet.

NEELY. I'm fucked up. I'm not insane.

DJ. Look I know how you feel but you can't take someone's kid.

NEELY. Alex's kid.

DJ. Regardless, you can't abduct a child-

NEELY. I think I should go.

DJ. To Alex-

NEELY. I juss hafta go.

(She picks up the crayfish and SOPHIE.)

DJ. If you stay here I promise I'll try to tell you what to do.

NEELY. No.

DJ. Please. I want you to stay.

NEELY. I swear I won't do nothin' stupid-

DJ. Please, Neely. I really don't want you to go.

NEELY. I'm gonna figure this out-

DJ. But we could do it-

NEELY. We can't. Cuz... Cuz I feel like you can see what I'm supposed ta be and I'm not that yet. Fuck, I'm messing everything up.

DJ. No you're not. I'm sorry for-

NEELY. No it wasn't meant that-

DJ. -making you feel that way.

NEELY. Thank you. *(Beat.)* Juss say, "for what?". Okay? You're supposed to say, "for what?". Please.

DJ. Neely-

NEELY. Juss say, "for what" okay? I need you to do that for me.

DJ. For what?

THE SECRET LIVES OF LOSERS

NEELY. For bein' a Snake on wheels n' lettin' me go n' not tellin' anyone about any of this.

(Beat. She turns to leave.)

DJ. Wait. You have to take the baby back. I promise I won't tell if you take the baby back.

NEELY. Promise. I'll bring her home.

(She turns to go.)

DJ. Neely.

NEELY. What?

DJ. If you don't come back... I... uhhh... I don't think I'll know why I'm here anymore.

NEELY. I- *(Beat.)* Berniece was a fuckin' idiot. *(She kisses him on the cheek.)* Bye.

(She leaves.Beat. DJ is alone.)

DJ. Bye Neely.

(Lights out.)

THE SECRET LIVES OF LOSERS

SCENE 16

(Same day. Lights up on NEELY'S living room. NELSON is on the couch. He wears a homemade t-shirt that says "Ask me how a ... " on the front. He is extremely high. The TV is on and blares "Wheel of Fortune". Next to the table is a can of gasoline. But the audience shouldn't notice it. The room is filled with the boxes of stuff NELSON found earlier. The table is littered with Corn Nuts, bottles of Yoo-Hoo and drug paraphernalia, plastic forks and matches. Postcards from all over the world litter the floor. NEELY is packing a backpack. The crayfish is on the floor near her. SOPHIE is on the couch next to NELSON. She cries.)

NELSON. Ohmigod ohmigod it's like a fuckin' is this Alex's- an all the shit I found it's like treasure day weekend-and during the *(Said like they do before the show.)* "Wheel- of-Fortune!!!" it's-

NEELY. Nelson be quiet okay-

NELSON. - it's oh shit- finals- big one- No dumbass don't use the the money for the that fuckin dog's not woof woof porcelain punkass -

NEELY. Nelson I'm trying to think-

NELSON. About the about the-

NEELY. Yes. Now if you could just be-

NELSON. Oooh... ooh lil baby —booya! Guess an R, R it is Ronald Reagan I knew it Vera from Rhode Island you have won-I've been thinkin' too you know like all day-

NEELY. Nelson just-can you-

NELSON. All day "gonna rock wit you-" you know that one I love that song been plannin' all day to that song-what're

you holdin'?

NEELY. What?

NELSON. What're ya holdin? Ya gotta pet?

NEELY. It's a crayfish.

NELSON. Crayfish.. Thass all so-yer so lucky-Can I hold it?

NEELY. Not- No-

NELSON. Please pretty please with sugar cherries on-

NEELY. What? Maybe. Later when yer not tweaked outta yer mind-

NELSON. Yeahyeahyeah- I just Mitchell scored like big winner I'm the top - but using it I've been being constructive-

NEELY. I believe you just can you at least turn off the TV-

NELSON. Big money big money- Bankrupt? Vera dumb bitch yer a dumb bitch like Sandra Shamas-Vera yer lettin' me-it was- you coulda' gotten-Fuck! The Tahiti trip Vera Tahiti-

NEELY. Turn the fucking TV off or I swear ta God I'm gonna break it-

(In the process she rattles the tank.)

NELSON. Suresuresure off like a prom dress hee... hee.. hee..

(He turns the TV off.)

NEELY. Oh Jesus sorry crayfish.

(She opens the tank and tries to put it back to normal.)

NELSON. Oh fuck I love so if you got that can I have the

baby as a mine like a pet that's mine-

NEELY. What?

NELSON. I could have her like a thing not a thing- like a baby- I could take- *(To SOPHIE.)* you would like that baby waybey-

NEELY. No Nelson I hafta-

NELSON. Me n' the kid we could be partners partners me n' the baby in crime like Johnny no Bonny no Johnny n' Clyde er whatever the fuck-

NEELY. No!

NELSON. You can't have two pets two pets is not fair-

NEELY. We're not keeping her.

NELSON. Then where is she going can I come too-

NEELY. Fuck. No. I can't take you.

NELSON. Thass right you can't thass okay cuz I had a sign so now I been plannin' plannin' thinkin' expandin' my scope with this plan ya see-

NEELY. That's great Nelson.

NELSON. Yeahyeahyeah... grrrrrr-eat like that tiger remember the tiger.

NEELY. Nelson I gotta go. I'm gonna take the baby okay?

NELSON. Okay thass okay cuz I got shit I gotta do-

NEELY. I know, I know. I gotta go though.

NELSON. Later skater.

NEELY. I'll try to call you from a payphone.

NELSON. Ooo shit you gotta plan too- I gotta plan and you gotta plan we both got-

NEELY. We do. *(She picks up the crayfish and SOPHIE.)* Goodbye Nelson.

NELSON. Yeahyeahyeah.

NEELY. No Nelson. Fer real goodbye like-

THE SECRET LIVES OF LOSERS

NELSON. *(He mimes a walkie-talkie.)* Rodger dodger ... hee... hee... rodger dodger. *(NEELY turns to leave. Miming the walkie- talkie.)* Neely? Come in Neely.

NEELY. What?

NELSON. Iss okay you been keepin' secrets captain.

NEELY. *(To herself.)* Fuck. *(To NELSON.)* Nelson I'm so sorry I never showed you her postcards-

NELSON. *(Miming the walkie- talkie.)* It's okay though cuz I gotta plan-

NEELY. I know you do. I bet it's the best plan in the whole world.

NELSON. *(Miming the walkie- talkie.)* I gotta plan and even though you won't let me keep her and you've got secrets I love you a lot a lot anyway forever.

(Beat.)

NEELY. Me too Nelson. I love you. A lot a lot. Forever.

(She turns and EXITS. NELSON turns around waving goodbye. We see the back of his shirt says "... winner feels".)

NELSON. *(Miming the walkie-talkie.)* You're gonna be proud Neel- when you come back yer gonna be proud of me swear to all the gods n' yer crayfish- over n' out.

(Lights out. In blackout we hear police sirens and fire trucks.)

THE SECRET LIVES OF LOSERS

EPILOGUE

(Same day three hours later. Lights up on the porch. ALEX paces back and forth extremely paranoid stoned.)

ALEX. *(Trying desperately to focus.)* Okay so if I was a baby... if I was a baby... a little baby waybe-shit focus man- if I was a baby and I walked away-wait-she can't walk- can she?- no she can't walk-so if I crawled away where would I go- no focus-she can't crawl- so if I rolled away-

(SYLVIA rushes on.)

SYLVIA. Ohmigod!

ALEX. *(Not realizing it's SYLVIA.)* Hey... *(To himself.)* Oh fuck! *(To SYLVIA.)* Hey.

SYLVIA. What's going on?

ALEX. Not... much... I have a little-

SYLVIA. Have you seen Neely?

ALEX. What? No.

SYLVIA. Cuz her brother is in so much shit.

ALEX. Huh?

SYLVIA. You haven't heard?

ALEX. No I've been-

SYLVIA. Her brother fuckin' set fire to Sunshine Estates and-

ALEX. The nursing home?

SYLVIA. Yeah. He piled all this miscellaneous shit in front of the building and lit it.

ALEX. Fuck!

SYLVIA. Yeah, the whole thing's burning. There's like five

THE SECRET LIVES OF LOSERS

fire trucks. All that polyester I'm surprised no one got killed.

ALEX. Jesus Christ.

SYLVIA. Not only that he fuckin' took all these postcards, forked them into the front lawn of their house in the shape of "fuck you", lit those too-

ALEX. Jesus-

SYLVIA. -and so not only is Sunshine Estates burning like a goddam birthday cake but so is the Neilsen house.

ALEX. Nelson burned down their house?

SYLVIA. I know. I know, he's crazy I mean someone should think about putting him away- Hey where's-

(DJ ENTERS in full uniform.)

DJ. Alex Richards?

ALEX. *(Under his breath.)* Fuck! *(To DJ.)* Officer I swear to god I-

SYLVIA. Officer Warren?

DJ. Oh. Sylvia.

ALEX. You know him?

SYLVIA. We've met. He's-

DJ. Look Sylvia it would be great to chat but-

SYLVIA. Is this about Neely's brother? Cuz it was totally fucked up what he did. I mean those old people-

(The following dialogue should be on top of one another yet still heard individually.)

ALEX. If my mom called Officer-

SYLVIA. -and their house-

ALEX. - I swear to fucking-

THE SECRET LIVES OF LOSERS

SYLVIA. -honestly I-

ALEX. -God I just stepped inside for-

SYLVIA. -thought Neely was a little fucked up-

ALEX. *(At the same time as SYLVIA.)* -a minute.

DJ. Have you seen her?

SYLVIA. -as well.

ALEX. Neely?

DJ. Yes.

ALEX. Earlier today. Holy fuck she wasn't in the house was she?

SYLVIA. Ever since the mother left that whole family's been downhill-

DJ. No, no, no one was in the house but- How's your kid?

SYLVIA. And really-

ALEX. Sophie?

SYLVIA. -someone should really-

DJ. Yeah, I guess Sophie-

SYLVIA. -think about putting her brother away.

ALEX. Ummm... She's you know... chillin'...

SYLVIA. Are you guys listening to me?

DJ and ALEX. Sylvia shut up!

SYLVIA. Jesus.

DJ. Your daughter's fine though?

ALEX. Uhhh... you know chillin' like a villain... Officer...

DJ. You sure?

ALEX. I'm her dad I think I would know where she is. Jesus, man.

SYLVIA. Where is she?

ALEX. Doing baby things Sylvia. Babies have things to do.

SYLVIA. What sort of things?

THE SECRET LIVES OF LOSERS

ALEX. Anything else Officer?

DJ. You're sure you haven't seen Neely recently like in the last couple of hours?

(The phone starts ringing.)

ALEX. Look man, cut the "Law and Order" act I told you I haven't. You've been hanging out with her. Don't you know where she is?

DJ. She was supposed to stop by here.

SYLVIA. Maybe she's coming over on her way home. Oh wait she doesn't have one anymore.

ALEX. Sylvia.

SYLVIA. What? It's true.

DJ. She said she would come by here.

ALEX. Well she didn't... Whatever. She'll be back soon and pissed as fuck.

(Beat.)

DJ. *(Realizing the state of things.)* Alex... She's not coming back.

ALEX. What're you talking about?

(We hear the answering machine.)

JESSICA. Al... Al...

ALEX. Fuck!

DJ. What?

SYLVIA. Who's that?

DJ. Neely?

ALEX. No it's Jessica dammit...
SYLVIA. Habbermyer?
DJ. Who?
ALEX. My girlfriend.
SYLVIA. Ex-girlfriend!
ALEX. Shhhh!
JESSICA. ... really fucked up... to just leave the fucking baby outside of my dorm room. We agreed- fuck! Is this like some kind of joke. We talked about this earlier. You know I have a life. I gotta get my grades- Alex- Alex if you're there and not answering. ALEX!!! What the hell am I supposed to do with her?

(The phone hangs up. Dial tone.)

ALEX. Fuck.

(Lights down. End of play.)

Also by Megan Mostyn-Brown...

girl.

Lizards...

CPSIA information can be obtained at www.ICGtesting.com
Printed in the USA
LVOW10s0252150316

479097LV00029B/1070/P